5TH DIMENSIONAL EARTH

JENNIFER LYNCH

5TH DIMENSIONAL EARTH

For all the brave souls who stood up for our freedom. I thank you.

CONTENTS

Breaking out of Illusion

Our fifth dimensional earth has been a long time coming despite parts of our earth reaching this vibration a long time ago. These were mainly limited to sacred sites which were maintained by small groups of evolved souls who knew how to use our earth's magic and energy grids. In general terms, earth's inhabitants have been stuck in the grips of the lower dimensions sometimes referred to as density, for centuries. We humans were unable to embrace change having had so little awareness of our true spiritual nature. No doubt throughout history, we've had some opportunities to evolve but it has been difficult to adjust our frequencies when we had no idea of the process involved. In addition, the dogma thrust on us through many religious practices taught us to worship God in the religious sense, rather than celebrating our divine spark within. Ultimately, this caused divisions between religion and spirituality which has remained for hundreds of years. If only we had awoken to our true potential earlier, the world would by now be a vastly different place.

Despite our lack of awareness and the denial of our personal power, we have lived alongside higher frequencies for decades. The angelic realms and their dominions along with many other high frequency beings have communicated to us throughout history, but their significance has largely remained misunderstood until more recent times. I believe this is because our hearts haven't been fully open to the many spheres of possibility. The consensus being that angels are fictional beings that exist in paintings, or are described in religious texts, but they don't have any relevance in modern day society.

How do we access the 5th Dimension?

Firstly, we must surrender to the idea that energetically, not everything may be as it appears. There is a need to embrace the value of our own spirituality (our light) and the importance of our higher connection. It's also important to acknowledge the concept of co-creation and our shift from the material world into group, or community consciousness, but hang on, haven't we had that before? To a certain extent, yes, but at that point in our evolution, there wasn't enough love on the planet to sustain it. The wars, particularly the first and second world war, caused divisions in humanity which took so long to heal that it's only now, while we are in yet another war, the war on consciousness that we've been given the opportunity to finally leave this density. The low dense vibration which has dominated the earth possibly since the middle-ages. We have been consumed by idealism, the pursuit of the American dream. The perfect family. The big house and pool. What's achievable if we can work long and hard enough to take out a massive mortgage but is the house that we've paid for ever really ours? Have we been working for the carrot that we can only enjoy in our retirement? After all that time will it have the same sweet taste when we finally reach our goal, or do we feel the bitterness of our struggle to make our monthly payments? Did the feeling of inequality and uncertainty cripple us because in life there are no guarantees, and our feeling of security had vanished in the process!

Consumerism is the biggest form of pollution on this planet, after electro-magnetic pollution, but that's a different book. It poisons everything in its path with its unfulfilled promises. We only need to look at the queue for fast food at a service station to realise how popular instant is. Food that's eaten with our fingers in throw away containers. Why would someone go for that, rather than buy a salad or something healthy to eat! Convenience has become part of our society. It works well with the rush, the latest mobile phone and the no need to take a break culture. In many businesses people seldom leave their desks. The lunch hour is now thirty minutes, being just enough time to eat lunch but there certainly isn't enough time to walk or clear your head. Communication has broken down. We are plugged into our phones, or the little white earpiece to obliterate the outside world. Fresh air has become dangerous, so has talking until it finally gets too much and we book an appointment with a therapist, then we can't stop!

In the seventies, when I was a teenager, and no doubt during earlier decades, families talked to each other. They made do with old, or second-hand things. I'm not saying that we should never buy something new, but people weren't obsessed with changing things for the latest acquisition. Do we ever stop to think if we like the latest, or if it's merely a must have. An essential, so we can fit. Yes, in the past there was a greater sense of community and people made the effort to talk to each other. They saw if they were well or needed help with anything. There is a need to return to that type of community because people seldom talk to each other, well, not in any depth. Many simply aren't interested in helping each other (I'm excluding my family and my amazing friends here!). If someone's discovered beaten on the street, some would prefer to take out their mobile phone and upload it to you tube rather than offer help! I remember many years ago when I had a head on car crash with a lorry, which was extremely traumatic, a lady appeared to ask if I was all right. I couldn't move but she suggested that I get out of the car because fuel had started to leak out. She said that she'd rung the fire brigade, but she couldn't hang about because there was no way she wanted to be called as a witness! I was horrified by her behaviour and terrified by my possible outcome which was looking grim! Fortunately, a whole fire crew very soon arrived to get me out. I was stuck because my car door wouldn't open. As much as I asked my body to move, the shock I experienced made it impossible despite the obvious danger I was in.

Contemplating on our current lack of sensitivity, has led me to believe that some people have closed their hearts? At times, physical presence and communication appear secondary to social media. Facebook, Twitter and Instagram, have become the new Gods, who fight each other for popularity. If we joined Facebook at forty, we were probably considered too old, so we set up your Instagram where all the youngsters who wanted to move away from their parents or grannies had disappeared to!

One of the popular uses of social media is a modern-day confession box, which works extremely well when we are emotional and want to offload. I told Facebook about it because I couldn't discuss my problems with my family and they found out anyway, along with hundreds of others! Our social media page even can live on after death as a memorial to us. Was it meant to be like this? Would people previously call, or send cards instead of the one-line message? What if we don't have social media? Do we still know what's appropriate? Or are we forever hiding behind screens. Has life become easier, or merely more convenient? We have the one good photograph which portrays our identity for our friends and followers, some of which we haven't a clue who they are, so we wonder why they bother! We can be temporarily lifted by newly made friends, with the occasional emoji, love, like, smiley, or virtual hug, aww! I'm not denying the importance of kind thoughts or saying that social media doesn't have a role to play but community appears to have broken down. Do you know anyone who was on their own last Christmas? How did we hear about it? Did we find out after the event? I was shocked to discover that some people I knew were alone, but I had no idea at the time because they didn't want to talk about it and appear vulnerable, besides they had the television and computer to keep them company! Have we lost the art of asking, 'Are you alright?' or, 'Is there anything I can do for you?' However, examining the failings of society isn't the sole intention of this book. Suffice to say that without the veil of the illusion being lifted, we will never see, awaken, or experience what's possible, our true divinity, purpose, and co-creation with God. How can we experience the divine within us when we are continuously distracted. Our illusions sit like a thick blanket and social media is just a corner of that! We could refer to it as a veil but in essence it's more of a permeating fog. It's only through intention and our willingness to venture that parts of that fog begin to lift, and we experience the light. We become aware and return to our spiritual nature, our divine essence, our sense of being. I wrote extensively about this in We Hear You Angels for anyone who would like to read my earlier book. Parts of this book are relevant to the shift in consciousness that we are going through now.

Awareness

There was a day, many years ago, when I suddenly became aware of the light. It was as if I had a lightbulb moment. A switch was turned on and I became illuminated. For the first time I was aware that there was something brilliant and bright accessible to me if I allowed it into my life. It wasn't inside a church, or in the street. It was wherever and whenever I wanted it to be. I guess that's what's meant by God is everywhere. I could see a column of light and almost summon that light to me through visualisation to experience its connection. Until this point, I didn't understand the light, which could be referred to as the light of God, or pure consciousness. For me it's both, we must be conscious, to be aware of its existence and to engage with it or experience it. My shift came for me in 1987 when my sister was ill with cancer. (More about this in We Hear You Angels). I had a vivid dream that I was looking through the top window of a church. I could hear the prayers of many people praying and healing her. I saw a vast column of light shining down on her body. I felt that I didn't need others to pray for me to activate my own light, I had to trust that I too was connected to something more powerful than I was presently experiencing. How many of us have had a death in the family, an accident, or a severe loss which nudged us in a new direction. We may have thought about our spirituality before, or we may have been partially aware, but we didn't have a clue how to engage with that part of us because it was closed off. It was something imaginary which was out of reach until something shifted to open the door to a different possibility.

The Church and Spirituality

For the first eight or so years of my life, I was brought up as a Catholic. I would say from the beginning, because I was baptised into the Catholic faith, having been adopted through the Catholic Children's Society in the sixties. As a child I feared religion, it terrified me. I remember looking at statues of Jesus in the Catholic Church in York, where I lived as a child, and I was horrified by the pain Jesus suffered. I found it strange that the women hid under black veils. It was almost as if they were ashamed, and I didn't understand it. Why was the service all about the father, son and holy ghost, when ghosts were something that we weren't allowed to talk about? I feel religion is something children find it difficult to comprehend. It's adults that understand it, or supposedly, because there are so many different levels of understanding. For me, religion is the result of an equation which has many formulars. If it works for you, it does, there's no judgement.

I believe our relationship with the higher power is personal, and it's something that we can choose to explore our whole lives, a single day, or not at all! Saying that, if you are reading this book, then you are likely interested in opening the door to different possibilities, or at the start of an awakening journey. However, anyone who wants to explore the light and penetrate the fog of the 3rd Dimension may quickly conclude that if spirituality is like religion, it won't be easy to decipher. Anything that's forced upon us with a lack of understanding, or learned parrot fashion, can feel like a punishment rather than a gift.

The Fifth Dimension is a gift to humanity, and it comes to us through our openness to receive. It appears on the edge of our reality, but for many, they may not feel it is part of them. It could so easily become so, if we choose to embrace the higher aspect of ourselves, often referred to as our divinity. It isn't something that has to be learned in the same way as studying biblical texts, but it does require us to slow down, stay present and count our blessings. As we evolve, we move through many different frequencies. We begin to retrieve lost aspects of us and through healing these aspects we become whole. We begin to embrace rather than punish. We are kind to ourselves, and we learn about self-love. Our ego no longer needs to control us because we are in trust. We return to the innocence of our child, and we learn to love and express unconditional love.

We are the Oneness of God

I recently mentioned to a friend that I authored a poem with this title many years ago, but I still believe this to be true. We are the oneness of God, the Divine, Universe. The greater aspect of us is inseparable from our essence. We are him. He is us. They are the same as us. We humans forget, make mistakes and sometimes find it hard to express ourselves but our higher self, our unique oneness with God, not the lower but the higher aspect of us, doesn't get things wrong. It's divine. It has light and connection with all things being part of God. The 5th dimension and beyond exist because there are many frequencies in the light spectrum beyond our human understanding. Perhaps we have ten fingers and toes for a reason, because God wanted us to expand by counting. We were given numbers because we as humans are so random that we need order to exist! God is orderly, because he created the heavens, along with the Orders of Angels. There have been many references to numbers in the Bible. I'm using the word God, as a reference but we could equally say the Universe, Divine, Higher Power etc. because words are energies that we created. Humans are constantly looking to understand God, or whatever reference we wish, so we can recognise the divinity which lies within us. Spirituality is both perplexing and transformational. It has also become essential at the time of our Earth's ascension (I will explain more about this later.)

Many have experienced seeing numbers as part of their awakening, 11.11, 22.22, or individual numbers. As many light beings are sent in to help Planet Earth evolve (love) which has the vibration of 6, some are using negative energies to reverse our progress. Numbers are powerful and can be used in both positive and negative ways! When I first became aware of 11.11, time stood still. The minute the clock took to move from 11.11 to 11.12 was incomprehensible, but for me, it was a karmic moment. Everything pointed to that time because the person I was with wanted me to become aware of it.

My friend brought me into his awareness, or his belief, so I could also experience the order of numbers. There have been many number moments since, particularly with the appearance of 444, the week two close family members died on consecutive days. This was a very tough time for me, and it was also the time when I saw an angel manifest in front of me. Shortly after I'd received this devastating news, I had to take my dog out. The angel appeared as a bright light which was in the shape of an angel. I followed this light, and I knew I wasn't alone, and it eventually disappeared, but it was proof to me that the angels were around me at an extremely low point in my life.

Despite having had some incredible spiritual experiences, I feel that it doesn't make sense to treat everything we see as a sign. If we continually look outside for confirmation of who we are, we may as well stop doing the inner work. Why bother to meditate to increase our balance and awareness, when everything can be handed to us on a plate? There are messages everywhere and the ego likes to go for the easy choice. Seeing eleven on a number plate means we are on the right track? I guess this is where people have the problem with some new age ideas. We are all guided whether we are aware of it or not, but it's up to us to learn how to navigate our internal compass. Looking back at my 11.11 moment, it felt as if time stood still! Could I extend time if I fully immersed myself in it? Being engaged in something, being fully present and no longer distracted, meant that I could achieve an awful lot more! Tasks that generally took ages to complete could be achieved rapidly. These points in time are bridges. They are mere snippets of what's available to us on a far greater scale. When we start to engage in the now, we align to our flow, our personal river because time doesn't have power over us. We have gained control, we've won. We have more space, freedom and we can achieve so much more, ultimate success. When we are fully present, we've gone beyond the waste of time, the pointlessness of past and future. Our inner compass is set and it's easy navigate! We don't need to recapture our past, churning it over like some bad movie in order to give us validation. We know who we are, instead of complying to multiple hats! We start to live a life of intention, 5D. We are purposeful and our drama, or story, no longer serve us! Our past is merely a set of building blocks that laid the foundations for who we are today, right now. The divine is supporting us through our growth. We can move forward at any chosen point. It's hard to imagine what's possible when we are burdened with baggage, but change can be instantaneous if we have a strong enough desire to be in the driving seat and we want to reclaim our power.

Feeling Empowered

Being empowered is about value. Do we love ourselves enough to support us during our spiritual awakening? Are we worth it? Can we be the change we want to see in the world? Are we our own best friend? This is precisely where we are! We're learning to live authentically. Some may choose to stay in the fog of self-denial, but why, we might ask? Because the uncomfortable has become comfortable and familiar however discordant, has become our cosy zone! Those who have risen above it, can see it for what it is, but for those who are living and breathing it, it's their reality. We must ask why we would bother to raise our vibration (frequency) if life is already good. We have a family, a car, a job, holidays and things are generally going well. Yet, two friends who have had a similar experience can view it entirely differently. We could go for lunch together and one of us could be completely immersed in how good it was, while the other spent the whole time picking away with a fork feeling it wasn't up to scratch! Is this because we were brought up differently and we've developed different attitudes or is it that one person literally sees something different to the other. Vibration is also about appreciation. The two are interlinked. I'm not saying that we should accept everything that doesn't resonate with us, but appreciation brings in love which opens the gateways to amazing things! We need to allow love to flow both to and from us. Giving and receiving need to be in balance.

Appreciation or Loss of Appetite

I'm sure at times, we've all suffered from an emotional loss of appetite. Life has become a little dull and boring. We can feel fed up with the people around us, or we feel stuck in the same old same old, whether it be our job, marriage or some other circumstance. If someone says to us at this point, try and move into appreciation, we might want to throw something at them, or saying, 'that's going to make a difference!' Yet, to move out of our self-created prisons, we must create a different energy or flow within us, particularly if we feel zapped, lethargic or uninspired, which is sometimes easier said than done. Look upon it as spiritual psychometry. We know that something exists, but we can't see it. To make the next stage of our path materialise (become part of our reality), we must give thanks for what we've already got! It can be quite simple things. Last year, for the second time in my life, I thought I was going to be homeless. This was ridiculous, because I'd already sold my home and I had enough money to buy another house, but could I find one? It was a lot harder than I envisaged. If it was just me, then it would have been easy to rent somewhere but now there were so many objections to having animals, it became obvious to me that renting wasn't an option. So, I had six months living with friends and I finally ended up with the dog in a caravan. The cat stayed in a luxury cattery!

I'm very grateful to the friends who helped me during this time because 2021 was an extremely challenging year for me along with still being partially locked down! My fear of being homeless during this time was immense. If I'd spent the money that I'd allocated to buy a house on staying in a hotel, then I wouldn't have had enough to buy a basic home and as I wasn't really working, I had doubts that I could get a small mortgage. I had started to live in a catch 22 situation which felt ironic, but what is catch 22?

'Catch 22 - A dilemma or difficult circumstance from which there is no escape because of mutually conflicting or dependent conditions.'- Definitions from Oxford Languages.

Considering 22 in numerology is a master number, I thought that catch 22 was lucky, but turn this on its head, it's a master number, so, the lesson was about mastery, which I learned as I went along. Fortunately, the people who came to my aid helped me with the process, for good or bad. I knew I was going through a huge transition, and I had to keep going however much I was challenged until I could see myself clear.

Some things happened that I would never repeat and yet others were a blessing, depending on my perspective. When the caravan I was living in was rocking from side to side, with rain pouring in through a window, after which I lost the electric, I felt helpless, but I also thought it was symbolic! I was powerless and out of control because I was placed in an unfamiliar situation. Having a home relates to our security on a very deep level. This is particularly hard for a Cancerian because we love our homes.

Where was my shell? I felt lost. I didn't know myself without that strong root, but I quickly concluded that I had to create a new root by finding new places to walk. There were many magical places particularly in Rendlesham Forest where I felt transported to a different dimension. As I explored the many paths in the forest, the trees became my home and protected me, and I awakened to a deeper connection with nature. I had experienced something similar many years ago when I lived next to some woods, but this time it had evolved to a whole new level. The forest brought about a feeling of contentment. Nothing seemed as bad as I first thought, and everything could be fixed. A few human angels appeared to help me who understood all about caravan pumps and the little place soon became livable.

Finely Tuned!

Our connection with nature is a huge part of our 5th dimensional shift. We cannot go higher without first expanding our root. That is if it is going higher? For vibration is just that, vibration. A frequency which is experienced within our body. Energy which pours into our chakras. Being in alignment so our emotions so they no longer pull us all over the place. A change in attitude, or belief which enables us to see clearly. The string of the instrument which has suddenly become finely tuned. Many people think ascension is about taking us to a place where everything looks different, but many of us have already been there for short periods of time. We often slip in and out of the higher frequencies because we want to exist in multiple dimensions. We love the familiarity off the fog! The stick that beats us up, that tells us we're not good enough. Empowerment and feeling deserving can be short lived when someone appears and presses a button that makes us feel uncomfortable. It could be a relationship, sibling rivalry, our own parenting, or many other situations that cause this, but we may feel that we've gone full circle. Are we still prepared to do the work to stay in the high vibration? Do we want to move into abundance and live at a higher frequency, enjoying the life we've created? I say create because we are still doing that now, through every single thought, even as I write this sentence, we are creating our future.

Our childhood wounds are obstacles that stop us standing in our power, a spoke in the wheel which slows us down and prevents our natural flow. The point at which we want change can appear obvious, but like children learning to walk, they fall over many times and progress can be slow. So, what can we do? How do we step into our channel and find a way of being that allows us to become part of the light, the integration, the completion of our stray parts that lead us to wholeness? For this to happen, first, we must heal the wounds of our inner child. This can be tough, and we may need a lot of help. We were born innocent, most of what we took on as a child was not by choice, but it can have influence over our whole life. We blame ourselves for so many things particularly circumstances that arose that we didn't understand. Situations that we took the blame for which weren't our fault. We hold onto that shame, which brings us pain. These things can appear minor in the eyes of others, but we may think about something that happened to us years ago and wish there had been a different outcome. One thing that I remember, about my childhood, was, that I was fed up with my parents ignoring me. They were probably plain exhausted and wanted us to go to bed. Apparently, every day, when my mother walked my older sister to school, I would sit on a pram seat on top of my younger sister's pram and fall to sleep. Then at ten o'clock at night when I was meant to be asleep, I would creep down the stairs by sliding down each step on my bottom, one stair at a time. I used to peep over the banister, and I could see my parents having their long-awaited supper! They'd have a bottle of wine with crackers and cheese. They would often leave the corkscrew lying on the table. The next morning after one of their suppers, when no-one was around, I noticed the corkscrew and decided to violently stab the coffee table several times. To this day I can still visualise the group of holes that I stabbed into it. I knew they'd be cross, and I didn't know what to do. When my mother saw it, she wasn't really that annoyed but they then started to put the corkscrew away!

I was angry. How dare they sit there every evening, laughing and having fun while I sat there all alone in the dark, too scared to tell them that I couldn't sleep.

My stabbing the coffee table incident stayed with me for many years. I felt guilty about the fact that I had tried to ruin their furniture. I guess that I held on to some of the shame surrounding it because as a child I couldn't explain why I did it. Children's actions are valid and shouldn't be punished. They have a desire to express their emotions and they often do things when ignored, separated or misunderstood. It's a cry for help. Inner child work isn't about blame, or shame. It's about healing the inner child. Releasing the child from that guilt, which was brought on through their lack of understanding. Thoughts and feelings need to be brought to the surface to allow the emotions to be released. We hold on to so much. We are heavy and weighed down by an anchor. We create our ball and chain! We don't want to be released from our traumas because staying in the victim is easier. We want to blame others because the truth can be painful, and releasing is very emotional.

Victim Consciousness

(I don't want to take responsibility for my own happiness!) Does this sound familiar? Years ago, someone told me that I was being a victim! Looking back at the circumstances now, I most definitely was! I was struggling financially, and I didn't want to take responsibility for my own life. Without going into detail, I found it unfair how things had worked out for me, and I wanted to blame other people and deny them what was rightfully theirs! I was revelling in being a victim and I stayed in that lower vibrational consciousness for quite a few years without admitting that I had any part in creating my circumstances.

Wallowing in self-pity is an easy thing to do but it's an awful lot harder to say, I need to change. I must accept things are what they are, and I'll work from that. Taking responsibility for situations is hard and is often something we don't want to do, but when we make the change, it creates a pulse of energy which sends a new message to the Universe. We become aware of what we have learned, and we move out of that 'poor me' scenario. The higher part of us is then in a different vibration so we are offered something better.

Whether this is the Universe's higher power or the more aware part of us, can be questioned, but trusting in the process rather than being in resistance to the process, plays an essential part in attracting positivity into our life. Having created the right space, we then need to ask ourselves what we want?

'What do I want? Something different, anything but not more of this!'

'Are we ready to take something else on? Step out of our comfort zone and feel that unfamiliar feeling? Perhaps feel a little uncomfortable with the new until it becomes integrated with who we are! Will we start to listen to the whisperings of our higher self and accept new opportunities that come our way, although they may not appear an exact fit? The perfect being something that often appears once we have moved out of our current mindset?'

'I'm in a state?'

'State it then. State what you want.'

'I want to move forward, anyway, anyhow.'

'So, would you ask someone for a job? Anyone, perhaps someone you know and prove yourself to both them and you.'

'I have and I did! For the first time in my life, I received the most amazing compliments.'

'You can sell snow to Eskimos.'

'I'll give you a job.'

'You are so good at this.'

'How are you are taking so much money at this event when no-one else is?'

During this time, my theory was, to cover my craft stand costs, I had to sell at least three of my sales products by 12 pm and the afternoon would take care of itself. Fortunately, after making such strong intentions, every time I attended these events, this is what happened. My expectations were met and because I was no longer a victim. I was taking responsibility, so my energy shifted.

I'm not saying that my personal story is

unique, but if we decide with power and conviction that we are going to re-write the script and create something else, we have the power to do so. Money is a form of energy. It's true to say that when we have money it can also energize us. As I mentioned previously, it's the power of freedom of choice. Being able to buy things that are important to us. Imagine retail therapy without money and we were given the opportunity to pick up whatever we wanted because life was plentiful and abundant. That's a little like living in 5D. It is in essence feeling that we will be provided for no matter what. That we are part of the source. Part of the creative process so that we can create from a place of worthiness not from a place of lack.

I moved out of lack because someone valued me enough to give me a sales job. It was a franchise and I worked independently which means more of the energy of my success flowed back to me. That time in my life gave me a huge sense of pride and achievement. Financially there may have been other ways of earning money but doing it yourself was incredible. Regarding communication, friendships, and challenges, my life was now both interesting and exciting and I'd started to live! I was no longer in the vibration of restriction. I was now in the vibration of flow, or the vibration of glow, besides, I could always sell snow to Eskimos!

In saying all this, I'm a healer and empath so of course I have compassion for people in difficult situations. I also work as an empowerment coach, and I help people grow. I see this as part of my work and soul path, and I have empowerment running as a theme throughout my books. How can we move forward if we don't believe in ourselves? We need to do this but it's hard unaided. It isn't always about hearing what we want to hear and ignoring the rest. We need to break the patterns by whatever means, taking a holiday, having a healing session, a discussion, counselling, whatever it takes. Being in the victim for extended periods of time is being unconscious. We are no longer aware of opportunity because we are fixed and there seems to be no place to go except that hamster wheel, the perpetuating cycle that we created. I've been in some circles, and I've arrived back at the same place. I was once told that it wasn't the same place because it was a level higher. Really, it looked familiar to me! I guess the fact that awareness is paramount to breaking that circular pattern and I was at least aware of the fact that I'd revisited! Hopefully, after we've done this a few times, we are free to move forward on a different course. It could appear to be a similar course, or one that is entirely different, but with more awareness. What will I look out for this time? When I see the signpost appear that says trust yourself, will I ignore it and slip back into my old familiar mindset of limiting beliefs. Who gave me these limiting beliefs? Are they serving me, or helping me to achieve my goals? They sound a little familiar. I can imagine them coming out of the mouths of my parents. It would be easy to blame them because I don't want to take responsibility! I learned it from them and now they've become my thoughts!

Are We Ready to Decide for Ourselves?

'She's an average so we'll put her in the B band, somewhere in the middle, not in the A band because she'll struggle.' I remember thinking why can't I say anything? Didn't I have some choice in this. They were talking about me! I wanted to struggle. I wanted to be with the brainy girls so they could help lift me up and I could prove myself. Seeing their achievements would make me work harder. I didn't want to find things easy, I wanted to be challenged. There was really nothing the matter with the B band, and I was told the children were happy there. However, after my father made this choice on my behalf, there I stayed. I was frustrated that I didn't have any input.

I was a late developer, and I took a 13 plus when I was 12 or 13. I can't remember much about it now, only the disappointment which followed. I was told that I had passed it but only a few children could be transferred to Grammar School, and I wasn't in that group. I didn't get to hear anything more. I was referred to as a late developer and I'm still developing now. Aren't we all? We are still learning in this lifetime of learning. The most I've ever learned is about spirituality and that wasn't on the school curriculum! If children aren't interested in the subject matter, they are going to be looking out of the window listening to the birds. I did, apart from when I had a crazy Irish Math's teacher who threw things at the kids who weren't paying attention and to be honest, I never understood math's. I think I skipped a few lessons preferring to walk around the school.

Math's and Science weren't my thing, but words were. I consider myself lucky to have been adopted into such a wonderful family with a mother and father who were both educated which gave me a huge advantage, but I was annoyed at being called an average. Labels stick like glue and very soon become our perceived identity. Our parent's thoughts, become our thoughts. Their limiting beliefs whatever it pertains to education, money, or opportunity become our reality. I told my children they could be anyone, do anything and they are doing this! I didn't mind what they did but they could achieve whatever they wanted. I wanted them to be limitless. There is no limit to the sky. It's vast. We create our own space, then we will fill that inner space with ideas. Our intentions enter the ethers and start to form. Just as much energy starts as a small seed before turning into something big. If your genie appeared to grant you a wish, would we wish in a small, limited way? Would we say to your genie, sorry, that's a little expensive? That dream is too big for me. He would laugh at us.

 'I've given you three wishes, and you've just wasted one because you don't feel worthy. Come on girl, dream big!' So, you look your genie in the eye and say to him, well actually what I'd really like is to be extremely successful and earn enough money to never work again.'

'That's two wishes. Sorry, you have already used two!'

'Ok, so I get another wish?'

'Yep,' he replies.

'I'd like to have my three wishes all over

again.'

'Why not? Now you're getting the hang of how this works!'

'Am I?'

'Yes, because you've realised there is no limitation. I've been waiting for someone like you. Don't you realise how horrible it is living in this lamp? You've let me go. I'm free. I was only here to serve you until you could create your own magic. It's a beautiful world in the 5th dimension. The birds are singing and there is a sweet aroma all around you. There are many guides who can help keep you on the right path but ultimately, it's up to you. Are you going to accept your labels or are you going to finally dispense of them?'

'Yes, they're gone. It's amazing. I suddenly feel quite different.'

'Awareness!' replied the genie and he vanished!

Forgiving our Parents

It's a tough job being a parent, let's not forget that! I've had so many fears in my lifetime, that I certainly can't blame my parents for the beliefs they subconsciously passed on to me. So many times, in the past, I've experienced huge money fears. I've had money, then not had any money, then had it again. Life has been a bit of a rollercoaster ride! I've truly experienced life's challenges. Money relates to the material realm, but it's also connected with our self-worth. At one time I felt that you couldn't be both spiritual and rich because money was a dirty thing that people don't really need. In essence, as explained earlier in this book, the energy of the fifth dimension is about being abundant and our ability to manifest anything but at this point where we are now, money still has relevance. It certainly isn't something we should fear because fear creates lack. We can be afraid of having it as well as being afraid of being without it. We are afraid of loss and afraid of gain. We may hold fears about having it then spending it too quickly. We may feel that we're undeserving. Do we draw comparisons between what's good spending. and what's bad spending? Why is that. Is there any difference? One thing that is for certain, when we get to the end of our lives we will undoubtedly look back and ask if we enjoyed it, in every way possible. It is doubtful that we will be happy about restriction. We will remember the times when we lived fearlessly, embracing different situations and challenges. When we smiled at our achievements against diversity. Wow, I've lived life to the full. No regrets. We won't even remember what held us back.

We may want to ask for our parents' approval. There is a part of us that longs to be accepted and the fear of losing that love is something that we wouldn't be able to bear. Yet, we are individuals who are born with our own challenges and set of circumstances. No-one else lives our life but us. Sometimes it is useful to look at our map of the world and realise that it is different from our parents for a reason. Individuality is a strength not a weakness. Setting ourselves free from former conditioning is essential for our growth and it is something to be embraced rather than frowned upon!

Can you still have wounds and awaken?

Let's look at this differently. Our wounds help us awaken. Our imperfections (although our soul is perfect) are necessary experiences, for us to grow. Often the pain of our wounds can bring us to the point where we don't want to carry, and we change direction. It can cause us so much pain. Just like a tree, when we reach the end of a branch and can go no further, that branch dies, and we return to the strength of the trunk. We eventually gather enough courage to move forward on our journey to find a new and stronger branch!

Our choices not only impact us, but they also affect others and the energy from those decisions quickly spreads. Sometimes within my work, I experience people who appear to have had the same set of circumstances and frustrations. I used to think it strange that so many were going through similar experiences at the same time but when we see the bigger picture, there is no coincidence. It is merely the collective consciousness trying to bring groups of people into a new understanding, perhaps through one of the universal laws. Presently the collective is on an accelerated course to bring as many people as possible to a new point of understanding. Our evolution is making a giant leap forward. While we are still dipping in and out of the higher dimensions the Angels and Ascended masters, who have agreed to help Earth currently, are appearing in our consciousness and dream states to guide us. Equally there are many opposing forces at work. There are enough light workers now, well over the required 144,000, a significantly small amount when we look at the population of the UK. These people are aware enough to help those who are struggling and are not yet living within the fifth dimension. So, it must be possible for us all to ascend, as we have a mathematical formular, if only it were that simple! We still need to surrender. While we are still fixed to the egoic behaviours of 3d, we will continue to dip in and out because it's impossible to do anything else. As I said earlier, we need to awaken to the fact that we have been living in illusion. We are not yet spiritually aware enough to create a new way of living which involves surrendering our ego identity to fully engage with the flow of what is, which is in essence, our true nature. I have struggled with this myself and it is only by being an open channel that I can access my true self and develop a greater understanding. What we create while we are in ego, are fences or barriers, which prevent us from seeing the truth and the light of our souls. The ego and all its counterparts will struggle to hold on in whatever way it can. It creates delusions, tells us untrue stories and hampers our progress at every opportunity. It is the mad monkey voice which condemns, sabotages the light and craves the trappings of the outer world. Essentially there is only one way of getting past our ego and that's through going within to develop awareness.

Awakening and my Story!

My awakening happened a long time ago. That doesn't mean I suddenly became aware of everything all in one go, but I experienced a profound change. I think the reason we awaken in stages, is so we can gradually assimilate the information which can appear so crazy, it's incomprehensible. When I started to have my realisations, (as I will call them because I'm sure there are many names), I started to see things completely differently. I was bombarded by images of things I had learned over the years in rapid succession. Stories from the news, things people had said, what I'd been taught at school, common assumptions, all sorts. It was like an explosion of truth. My logical mind was saying, no, surely not, but they kept on coming and the illusion, or the fog, began to thin and I was able to see much further! This could be described as the 3rd dimension breaking up. Perhaps we've been aware of this? Were there also weird geometric shapes or squiggles, like tuning into another channel on a television set!

The change in me happened one weekend when I insisted on dragging my then husband, a Bonsai stand, and boxes of complaining trees, to the Halls in Norwich. I'm unsure of the year, but I would guess it was 93 – 95, or maybe a bit earlier. There I was with my stand all set up in a very ancient church in the centre of Norwich at a Mind Body & Spirit event. Primarily, I wanted to hear David Icke speak. This was one of his first round of talks and his audience was small, about 35 people! I was next to his wife all weekend. I assume it was his first wife Linda, who was busy selling signed copies of one of his early books, Robots Rebellion, and I was fascinated. I must confess that I've still not read the book, although I have several of David's earlier books about spirituality, and I've watched endless footage of his talks on you tube. Hearing David is a shell shocking experience when we become aware of the lies that we've been fed. He always includes the spiritual. He has a deep understanding of how our energy systems work. In those days people didn't refer to the matrix, mainly because the movie hadn't been released but now it has created more awareness with constant referrals to the red pill!

After talking to Linda most of the weekend, I then returned to my very normal life, having only sold one Bonsai tree all weekend. The general opinion was that they didn't fit well with a Mind Body Spirit Event because they were poor tortured little trees, and why didn't I realise that trees had feelings! I was perplexed as I saw a man who had been openly snorting white powder all weekend and I wondered if he was more tortured than our bonsai!

The weekend event was an eye-opening experience. My husband declared that it was a complete waste of time and why would I want to hang around with people in rainbow coloured clothing, who had lost the plot! But I was shaken to the core by the information I'd discovered, the political lies, the illusion, the New World Order and how we were being manipulated. I remember the

Robots Rebellion lady giving me her number and I called her and spoke for over an hour. 'Isn't there anyone else you can talk to about this,' she asked?' I remember replying, no I haven't, but I met many like-minded souls that I could turn to a few years later. In fact, there are many stories of how my soul group started to appear and I was friends with some of them for years. When we shared our stories, I discovered we were at the same places at the same time, although at that stage we hadn't been aware of each other. They were also from the thirty odd people who went to listen to David. My soul group were already walking simultaneous paths, but we hadn't acknowledged each other. Yet, it was essential that I met with these people because they were at the next stage of my awakening process, and I was in for more surprises.

Is Being Awake Different to Being Spiritual?

There is no doubt in my mind that awakening is spiritual, although people may disagree with me! Spiritual people are concerned with love, caring, freedom, and sovereignty. What is sovereign? (There are so many connotations of this). It depends which source of information we consult! Many relate it to being regal, as King, Queen, and others anti-government. For this book which is intended to be about the shift and not solely political, let us replace sovereignty, freedom and human rights, our connection with the earth, mother nature and identity as an individual in oppose to globalism.

Being sovereign means that we want to be part of a system which honours and supports growth and empowerment, i.e., a fair system, the original common law. Having a government or Authority that doesn't subject us to excessive taxation or being coerced or mandated through a fear agenda. A short while ago, I found it impossible to see how being sovereign had anything to do with spirituality, yet the common laws of the land have been eroded to such an extent that our constitution has lost its original significance which was to protect the people.

The King is sovereign because he has a duty to protect the people from corrupt Governments. Many wish to return to this Common Law (original law) because they're looking for a fairer system, not one which is influenced by large corporations. Our individuality is being eradicated. We are losing our sense of identity because we are being filtered through a sieve until there is nothing left. There are new rules wherever we look, and many are completely bonkers. Notices displayed that have nothing to do with the law, which were created by corporations. Landowners who dress and look like Police Officers and Traffic Wardens. The world has become a very confusing place. As I write this book, we are on the brink of a One World Government and digital currency. The farming industry has been dominated by the World Economic Forum under the guise of climate change which has destroyed small farming communities. Our food chains have been tampered with and large areas of land have been bought up by the global elites so they can dominate our food chains with GM crops.

Existing in the third dimension, has created loss of freedoms through excessive enterprise, so it's hardly surprising that there is a strong desire for many to return to nature, to a simpler way of living. To live in communities where people share their daily work, and farm their own land, while it's still possible! We are currently living in a system that has malfunctioned at the deepest level. Many people no longer want to work. They have given up. I've heard some companies in the U.S are paying people to attend interviews. What went wrong? Since covid and the lockdowns there is no longer a desire to travel to work and be stuck in the 3d matrix, 9 to 5, work to survive. We want the freedom of working from home or self-employment. Can we blame people for this.

Our governments squeezed us so hard; we ran out of juice! The old ways no longer work. We must return to the land, community and the values of our ancestors, to feel our worth and not be given jobs that have no security. We must rebuild trust because our politicians have destroyed any resemblance of faith! We still want our freedom. The right to roam. It is part of both our heritage and sovereignty.

Covid and the Lockdowns

Covid 19 and the lockdowns were interesting. Presently we are still experiencing an attack on human rights, and civil liberties in the name of Covid, despite some great doctors and politicians who have tried endlessly to awaken us to the truth! Personally, I believe there is a virus called Covid, as in the illness. Why, or how we have it, we may never entirely know. Was it released on the human population, so we'd subscribe to something bigger, or it was the result of a sick experiment that got out of hand, or a combination of both? Whatever the reason, there is no doubt the virus will continue to mutate. It will adapt to our modern day living and revisit us in different forms, as does the flu. I'm not a scientist but a channel, at this time in Earth's evolution, I'd ask you to listen to your heart and not your head. The higher dimensional beings say this.

We are here to help the transition to the 5th

dimension, the upgrade for planet earth but many dark entities still roam the planet and want to stop this happening. The prison of 3d is spiritual, environmental and political. Toxicity is as catching as positivity. Fear is our greatest enemy, and it is solely through this negative emotion, that we become stuck in the 3rd dimension, the fourth being more positive because the light has started to penetrate but much remains as theory. While in the 4th density, the 5th remains a story of what others believe without any scientific facts! It could be possible but then again, it's easier to believe in what already exists, the how could there be an alternative truth? Struggle and fear, sabotage and pain, trying and failing we willingly subscribed to this. How could trusting in the process work, that's ridiculous! Are we that naïve? Being present is fine but who does that?

The 3rd dimension is about being fixed where rigidity, anger and denial play strong roles. In the 5th we can create our own reality. As explained earlier, when I talked about wanting to step into the driving seat, by this stage, we are already in the driving seat because we have started to take control of our own destiny! We may occasionally need help but much of the time we are guided by a sense of trust and ultimate surrender. If we are living within the 5th dimension, it's unlikely that we won't worry that much about covid, because we will already be living in a frequency beyond illness and as such, exercising some form of self-mastery, through meditation or other spiritual practices. Having something alien injected into us, that's still a trial, wouldn't fit with who we are. I know for some this may appear weird. It may be ridiculous to think that we are protected from something that is running riot in the 3rd dimension, but we would have already agreed to this on a higher level before we stepped into our role (in this earth life) not to undertake the negative aspects of this. It's almost as if Covid has come into our lives to challenge our fear. To see if we can raise our frequency high enough to surpass it, or to be drawn into the fear of the dis-ease which quickly manifests into the physical. In saying this, I'm certainly not suggesting that anyone who contracts covid is less spiritual,

I'm sure that many people have agreed to take this on, in order to show others something and at the same time to detox their system! We exist as vessels for the divine to channel the higher energies. By keeping our channel clear it allows us to receive insights and illumination and our bodies are still healthy and pain free. If we allow pain, not through our conscious choice but through our soul wishing to gain greater insight, this can also be illuminating. As I explained earlier, we also awaken from our suffering. As humanity suffers through covid, the actions of those who suppressed and censored the truth will eventually also awaken and humanity will grow. They cannot hold onto something that is destructive to man/womankind without revealing the origins. We chose to be here at this time as someone who needs to experience the dis-ease, or another with strong political views, who could say that it doesn't exist. Most people who have eyes to see can't deny that while all this was going on our government has been eroding our human rights.

Fortunately, or unfortunately, the spiritual dimensional world isn't concerned with right or wrong. The way forward is through balance, not just of individuals, or as some may say the scales of justice or law of karma, until we reach the vibration where there is no longer a need for duality. Our higher dimensional frequencies become available through realization, but has the person who suffered through terrible mistakes, illness, or otherwise, then not been able to access the higher dimensional reality because they don't deserve it? Are they not good enough because they didn't understand, or perhaps they didn't awaken others? That isn't how it works! The energy frequencies are interchangeable. We don't exist merely in one dimension because there are many overlaps. Most people have already experienced the 5th dimension on some level. It's the level of bliss and many of us have been there at some time, or another even if it was short lived. It could have been through human contact, a birthday, a fantastic holiday, a fairground ride, receiving our degree. There are many situations that bring us into pure joy. What's happening now is that the bliss vibration has become more accessible to us as the overlaps between the dimensions are permeable. We can literally walk from one frequency to another at will. We have discovered the love inside ourselves which allows us to walk through the houses of God, (many mansions). We have had opportunities to increase our awareness (as the collective consciousness of humanity) but as explained earlier, until now, there wasn't enough love on the planet. There had to be a certain amount of people who had already shifted into the higher frequencies before this could happen and our old world began to collapse. Self-love, value and empowerment were considered wrong by some elements of the Church. We were born sinners being impure and we were given a lifetime to prove ourselves to God. Since many people are now stepping up, healing their childhood wounds and moving into self-love, this has helped humanity to awaken and shift into the 5th dimension. The gateway to universal love can be experienced by many, not just the lightworkers, but anyone who needs this love. Healers both healing and being healed are evolving so they can have a greater understanding. This is where the Angels step in to help and direct that love and to work with individuals who have agreed to collaborate with them through a soul contract. This isn't everybody's mission. There are many missions which are all equal important!

How can we remain in the Fifth Dimension?

Being mindful, staying present and not allowing our mind's mad monkey to run riot is easier said than done! We seem to have lost the ability to do one thing at a time in our fast-paced world. People are expected to work crazy hours on smallest hour contracts when minimum doesn't really exist! It's more about modern day slavery. We either have a job and we're over worked or struggling to find something and had to go onto Universal Credit. The amount of money which we'll receive is never going to cover our basic expenses. It's a joke! We need a fairer system and there will be a fair system soon. People are juggling so much, work, kids, family life, if we are not a good multitasker or we don't. We're expected to hit the ground running, or we will be made to feel slow, inadequate and we'll soon be replaced by someone who is automated enough to be able to cope with that. I once did a temporary job where I couldn't understand how to use this fax machine, apparently there was a code that I had to put in to retrieve the faxes. At the end of the week, I was heavily criticized for not retrieving them. I was meant to read the instructions on the wall, but no-one told me that, so I assumed we didn't have any faxes. This was a moment in my life when I decided that I wasn't a great multi-tasker, but the reality of the situation is that I'm dyslexic and therefore I sometimes find reading and following instructions extremely hard. Multi-tasking was a kind of office buzz word for a while, until it was replaced by hit the ground running! I wonder what will be next. Sensitive souls find fitting into boxes or categories extremely difficult because many of us just don't! We're all here for different reasons. Some of us are healers and light workers and we don't fit the mould of anything else that well. There's no doubt that we could all succumb to a certain amount of parrot training but becoming automated wasn't what we signed up for. We are here to help others, grow and evolve. I wonder if when I stood up and said that I wasn't putting up with this and drove out of the car park, anyone grew. I knew that I'd be wasting my time explaining that I wasn't automated because the third dimension was created to do this! Pick up the speed go faster, or I'm out. Why can't I remember everyone's name? What's wrong with me? I was crushed but I wasn't broken. I had to earn money to look after my family, and I was beating my head up against the brick wall. I realised that I was asking the wrong question. I needed something that would fit, I had outgrown the overcoat that I was hiding in. Why wouldn't I cast it aside, was I scared to be me. I was suddenly back in the classroom with the other children they called remedials (in the 60s). I wasn't like them. I could read everything, but I couldn't say get the words out. Why couldn't I communicate and show people that I was intelligent. I knew I could do it, but no words came out. I had a block, and I just wanted a chance! Why was I different?

Warriors of the Rainbow

In more recent years, I have often said, thank God we're not all the same. We are the warriors of the rainbow, and we have many colours. Now is the time to step into our warrior self and express our own individuality, showing people our true colours. It's not time to hold back and hide our light! We must step forward and communicate, chant, heal, meditate and sink our roots into the earth. As above so below. It's time to bring heaven to earth. The shift is about allowing more photon light in through a process of photosynthesis. Yes, humans can do this, they already do it with sunlight and vitamin D. It is almost like a small nuclear re-action as the light re-acts with each of our cells. We are being re-generated, changed. Our DNA is being upgraded. As a result, we will experience better health and a longer life. Part of our upgrade is, that we will no longer have the desire to eat animals. Many are already doing this, they have changed from meat eaters to vegetarians and now many of us are vegan, eating plant-based products. There will be a different code of ethics based around the heart. Our earth heart connection is growing, stabilising and in a sense grounding us into mother earth because we are at last listening. As the earth aligns, we too become centred, and we can reclaim what we've lost. Our environment, our community and our voice. After the devastation and the end of tyranny, there will no longer be separation. The biggest change will be co-operation and a willingness to re-invent our social structures in new and positive ways. Being sovereign means that we want to oversee our own bodies. We will reject branding and see the unprecedented evil that has consumed our planet particularly in the last 3 years. There will be new systems and new medical alliances where natural health is treated with the same importance as any other health system. Many who do not want to be part of the new earth vibration will choose to remain trapped within the 3d, fearing change but eventually as more systems collapse, there will be little choice but to embrace the new opportunities which are being created by the souls who incarnated for this purpose. They know who they are! We will live in equality and wealth because poverty consciousness will no longer exist. People will be conscious and act in fair and indiscriminate ways. Most things will be free and exchanged, so tasks will still be done through our willingness to co-operate plus a desire to build new forms of community.

Poverty Consciousness and Money

There is so much fear around money. It has been a cause of so much disruption on this planet ever since it came into being. It creates the illusion that some important things have no value and other things which should be less valuable are ridiculously priced. One of the worst things is that we half kill ourselves to have more of it. While some people are just dead lucky at attracting wealth, others find that it easily slips through their fingers. Our belief systems about money are often handed down from our parents, or through not clearing situations from our past lives. Some of us are taught to save money, while others learn how to spend it. Some believe that money comes to us easy come, easy go, and others hold onto it in tight fisted ways because they strongly believe that if they spend it, it won't come back. It's a joke to say money grows on trees, yet, anything is possible, is part of the Fifth Dimension, being limitless. It involves focusing our intention, then letting go. We need to honour the process that whatever we let go of, will flow back to us for our highest good. Do we stop our flow because we unable to embrace receiving? Can we believe that when we align to our soul purpose, everything will flow towards us including money? Why are we here now if it isn't for us to learn this? When we are worrying, we are out of our true vibration and emitting something entirely different, a lower frequency which isn't responding to our greatest intention. So, if we set an intention and sabotage it, by worrying, how can we expect to manifest when our infinite space has been taken up with worry, rather than allowing that energy to transmute and fill our vessel with what we wish to receive!

5D is about unified consciousness. Unified consciousness is both one and many. There is no distinction. Beyond the 3rd and 4th dimensions money starts to be irrelevant, the process of manifestation means we can attract what we need without it and if everyone was without it, then it would literally mean the desire for the objective thing that keeps us within these dimensions would disappear. 5D is about letting go and trusting the solutions will appear with or without money. Money is not the only path to your desires. It was created in inequality. Therefore, it has remained that way and for some it doesn't matter how hard they work, they are incapable of making their ends meet, whereas others don't know what to do with everything they've accumulated! They can buy things which bring them short term happiness, but the riches they experience in their inner world would bring greater wealth. So, the question is still, do we have to feel rich, to be rich? What is rich? Wealth has little to do with money! We can be rich in our health, family, and happiness, that's abundance. If we believe that we are already abundant, then we'll attract more positive situations to us. More love, better friendships, people who are there for us in our lives, priceless people. Feel the love from those friendships. Embrace gratitude because it allows the gateway to open. I'd love to work as a full-time writer and I'm creating the abundance for this process. It isn't about my monthly income, rather the fact that we acknowledge our desire to be part of the greater consciousness, then we are vibrating within it. By holding our positive intention, we are saying what we wish to co-create within the unified field. This field is constantly expanding to incorporate our willingness. In a sense it's a superbeing that grows in understanding as we accept it, therefore it begins to accept us, and it manifests. Sometimes it responds to us almost at once, other times we must wait. Our belief that our desires aren't instantaneous, and we have to work hard at achieving, can cause a time lapse, rather like a neurotransmitter trying to jump across a synapse to deliver a new message but there is a block in the receptor. The jump appears larger and the re-action slower because of our analytical nature. Our minds often say, no we can't have it. we don't deserve it because we haven't worked hard enough, so adapting to the fact that something is instantly achievable is alien to us, but that is the prison of the 3rd dimension. We chose for it to be this way through our limitation. We don't want to oversee our own power, our lives, our bodies. We gave that away to our masters. The matrix is our comfort zone where we continually give away control and power. We were trained for this from the moment we were born. We'd already given away our identity as we entered a series of numbers which became our identifier, our birth certificate. How far do we want to let this go?

The Matrix

The matrix is a prison x marks the spot. It's the spot where we are paralysed by indecision, and we have in a sense lost our direction and purpose. At this time in our evolution, we are being given the opportunity to step out of illusion and rely on ourselves, our internal system, our intuition and to use our critical thinking to find new ways forward. We have come to realise that it isn't necessary to follow the ways of others if our critical thinking says no, that's not right for me. Our desire to express our individuality has become paramount for our soul's evolution. Many of us have incarnated for this reason, and as explained earlier, we are drawn towards our soul groups. We will feel like we intuitively know these souls because they understand us effortlessly, and we speak the same language, by that I mean that we feel and talk about the same things. Some will have healing gifts or work dimensionally by using light language and other mediums which are now being understood as they are part of our healing. The divine connectiveness of light, which is a living breathing organism, pulsates with light, from which we can channel messages (as in this book) or heal what's out of balance. Healing intentions are like a ripple, or wave throughout the universe which is received and fed back through the circuits of light which surround the planet. The energy grid that we are part of (not the matrix) the interconnectedness of all things. Our intentions are pulses of light which are part of our original blueprint. The map of who we are, and why we are here. Everyone having a significant role in the evolution of the planet. We can also have unintentional intentions! What, I know that's crazy! We can put out a pulse of energy to the grid which says, we want something that we don't. We must be incredibly careful what we ask for because our thoughts are energy. We can create in Godlike ways, but we can also self-sabotage. Becoming aware through meditation, can keep away our negative thoughts, and wrongful intentions, under control. If we make a mistake, we can correct it, but we will need a new message, something stronger, which overrides the negativity. We are in control. We were never expected to be perfect. We make mistakes but we can also correct things. Consciousness is everything. It is so important that we stay present. Ultimately, we will come to realise that being present, is a gift!

Reality v non-reality –

Are we Living in Simulation?

How can we believe in a positive outcome when on some level we don't believe it? Reality is subjective. There's simply no point in stating to someone that something's real, or unreal, if it's impacting their life in a dramatic way, because they will believe their version! Belief systems and resistance to change is multi-layered and often evidence based. In other words, we see the evidence we wish to see. If someone approached us with an alternative viewpoint, while we are existing mainly in 3rd density and suggested that things could be entirely different, if shifted our thinking, it is likely that we would experience a very negative response. The matrix (3d prison) is as real as a mental prison. Everything we experience in 3d is connected to cause and effect. I once had my hair cut in a salon by a young female hairdresser who was friends with a man I was dating. This man wasn't divorced and there but there was little chance of reconciliation between him and his wife. Despite this, I knew that the attraction I had to him was unhealthy and a waste of time because he hadn't had enough time to heal that relationship. I knew I was a bit of light entertainment for him and, I could never see myself with this man long term, but even with this awareness, I couldn't stop the pull!

I arrived at the hair salon with the pleasant feeling that I was having a complete day off. Being a single parent and the mother of two teenage boys, I hadn't bothered with any makeup because I was having my hair washed anyway. As I sat there viewing myself in the mirror, I thought that I looked washed out and unattractive, and I wondered why I came to this salon. I knew that the hairdresser who had been recommended to me was friends with the wife, so why did I take his advice. She was a good hairdresser but there were many good ones in our small town, and I suddenly felt extremely uncomfortable. I had such little self-love at the time. If I had been kind to myself, I might have thought, oh, well I looked tired but not unattractive and soon I would have lovely hair which would perk me up!

Sometime later I saw the man I'd been dating in the street. He'd moved onto someone else, behind my back, but we still occasionally spoke. He asked about my hair and how I got on in the salon which was now weeks ago. I said that I was pleased with the hair cut and I was glad I'd gone. At this point he told me that the young hairdresser had said something nasty about me. I was shocked by this, and I felt kind of set up by the man. I pressed him to see what she said. 'She told my wife you were ugly,' he said with a straight face.

I thought I looked terrible on that day, so what he said was a complete reflection of my own thoughts. I wondered why he was being so childish, and that he felt the need to tell me this. But I also realised that I'd asked for it! The situation felt very karmic, and it was a huge lesson. His comment didn't impact me that much, but his lack of empathy did. I was a tired single parent, and it was obvious that he didn't understand!

I've had many examples of cause and effect, but if we don't learn from these lessons, we remain stuck. Try explaining to someone who has just been through that, that the situation manifested through lack of self-love, rather than anything about our appearance. It could certainly be challenging!

We're given many opportunities to change, to evolve and to love. Some very evolved souls say, thank you for that experience. I must confess to being particularly bad at that, probably because I'm a Cancerian, a sensitive tenacious crab, but I am aware that through these experiences we are able to remove a bar from our windows. We can start to see the light of our soul. When we step away from something that isn't right for us, we can see its density but when we are in it, that magnetic attraction pulls us further towards it. It can appear as the shoe that's the perfect fit but all we are seeing in these interactions are the parts of us that are desperate to be healed. It's an opportunity to be free. We subconsciously asked for the perfect set of circumstances to heal that deep wound that was stuck in a vibration where we still had an energy attachment. We wanted to graduate but we were living in two different realities. How can we be over there and over here at the same time? How can I believe two sets of circumstances, it's creating such a division inside me, but I must because I don't want to upset my friends? If I'm true to myself, I will lose them. I am not really a people pleaser! How do I change this. Is what others want more important than my own needs? I remember I was never really an average, and I've dispensed with that label. Yes, what I want matters, I'm not someone's opinion of me. I am me and I am free to be me!

Two Camps Neither Comfortable

To take that evolutionary leap into 5th Dimensional awareness, we must learn to honour ourselves. It's great to be what everyone expects of us, but it can diminish our energy and we'll end up becoming a shadow of our former self! How many hats are we wearing? Do we enjoy being less than we are? Does being subservient help us. In saying this, I'm not saying that being humble doesn't have a role, apologising and acknowledging that we aren't always right is a strength. Humility is an endearing quality which is far superior to arrogance! However, to transcend the third dimension, we'll need to be us and allow the energies to flow freely through our chakras. I've been the woman with too many hats. I used to think the hats that belonged to others, looked better than my own, so I was constantly seeking new ones! But when I looked at my vast collection of all the people I pretended to be, I would move into total brain fog. It felt as if nothing was clear. Was I just a parrot? Had I taken on the words and attitudes of others? Where was my voice? What do I want to say? Thinking back, this all started with my dyslexia when I first learned to read and write. I can only describe it as me, the real me was shut in some kind of box with a closed lid, which I visited in my dream space. I had the numbers, the codes to re-open the box but I couldn't remember them. This could be past life, future life, soul memory but it was important to my mission and why I came to planet earth at the time I did. I was told in my twenties that I would be part of a peace movement. I didn't understand what it was about but now it makes a lot of sense. 5D is a peace movement and we all hold a piece of the puzzle. We are not separate beings we are one huge organic being and we are all interconnected. What we do, what we say, or what we think is a vibration that not only influences other people, but it influences our environment.

I had this fascinating dream which I'm remembering right now, as I write, about my country England, breaking in half. My friend and I were on rope ladders trying to cross from one side to the other, literally its backbone had parted! As I crossed the chasm, I was afraid, I thought that I would fall but I kept going. The fact that I was willing to cross this massive crack was part of the healing process. The dream didn't make much sense at the time. Now with the split in our society, it's much clearer. We as lightworkers are literally putting our lives at risk to try and stop this division, this split in society. The wound that can only be healed through love. Are we going to allow our politicians to divide us from our family and friends, or will we unite and work together to create a fair and more equal world? Can we stand together with our sovereign hearts and embrace the energy of the 5th dimension? Can we ascend to a light dimension where we're not controlled, emotionally raped or tortured? We are love, pure love. Our hearts are pure and as we step into the light of our consciousness, we see no divisions.

Can we hold that energy now and fill our bodies with divine light, or will we remain in the dark energy of fear? The collective shadow. The shadow that humanity needed to experience to heal our darkness, which has been misunderstood. We're at the brink of the highest evolutionary jump in human history but we're still adding to the shadow. Can we see beyond it, that it's our sorrow, pain, vanity and ego, our need for identification with the physical, which is causing the cracks, the chasm where we can only reach each other with unstable mental ladders. Are we willing to sacrifice our friends, neighbours and colleagues because they don't share the same views as we, or will we step into love? Will we surrender to our higher guidance and accept that although we may not agree, we won't ridicule their beliefs. As love increases within, we, we then become an aspect of love. The light which was once unobtainable to us merges with us and we carry that column within, giving us strength and understanding. The light radiates its message as we form groups. Many souls are reuniting currently for this reason. We are all natural co-creators, and we chose to be here now!

About me and my links

Jennifer Lynch is the author of several books which include, We Hear You Angels, The Silver Lining, William's Wishes, Never to be Told, Liberty Angel, Salsa, Attracting What You Really Want (eBook), Shades of Kefalonia which is also available as an audio book. She works as an Empowerment Coach and gives Angel Card Readings working at home and throughout Suffolk, Norfolk, Essex and Cambridgeshire.

She has a show on Blog Talk Radio called the Natural Co-Creators Show along with interviews on her you tube channel, Natural Co-Creators and Angel Wisdom. More details about Jennifer's work can be found on her website angelwisdom.co.uk
Visit and join her Natural Co-Creators Community on Facebook. Jennifer's books help with our inner journey empowering us to move into wholeness. We Hear You Angels Jennifer's most recent book, includes information about the Archangels, meditations for release and messages from

the Angels for humanity. We are at a particularly crucial time in earth's evolution. People are connecting to angels currently as they wish to help us in our ascension process.

Shades of Kefalonia is a short book of meditations which Jennifer wrote during her stay in Kefalonia. They are primarily about colour and the chakras. There is also an audio book available via Jennifer's website which can be downloaded as a whole or individual tracks.

Jennifer's books are part of her own healing journey and part of the journey the evolvement of humanity. Please enjoy them and review.
Interviews: - BBC Radio Suffolk - The Lesley Dolphin Show - Skin Deep now William's Wishes and Liberty Angel where Jennifer discussed Angels with Lesley.

All my books including the Silver Lining, were discussed with Tom Evans- on The Zone Show
A series of Archangel Articles from We Hear

You Angels were featured in the extremely popular Universal Magazine.

Meditations from Shades of Kefalonia were featured in (September 2015 edition) of Kindred Spirit.

Jennifer's website
is www.angelwisdom.co.uk where you can find out details about her Angel Readings and therapies and her events.

My Facebook Group - Natural Co-Creators Community Group

Printed in Great Britain
by Amazon